When sunflov

A collection of poetry a

By Yasmin Ilahi

Copyright © 2020 Yasmin Ilahi

ISBN: 9798576509539

All rights reserved, including the right to reproduce this book, or portions thereof in any form. No part of this text may be reproduced, transmitted, downloaded, decompiled, reverse engineered, or stored, in any form or introduced into any information storage and retrieval system, in any form or by any means, whether electronic or mechanical without the express written permission of the author.

Contents

When sunflowers sing 1- 23

Lavender Fields 24 -60

The Sunflower

Paradise garden, green and lush. Berries a sharp red growing on a bush.
Translucent petals fall like the autumn leaves, golden with a dash of hazel.
Immense beauty beyond belief.

A flitted ray of yellow beams down so bright. Elegant, light standing tall, each petal a honey-suckled yellow. The bird of paradise standing tall, for all to see. Her beauty speaks to me. Singing in the morning hour.

When sunflowers sing

Your kisses are as gentle as the morning rainfall.
Your smile is as beautiful as a yellow sunset.
You make me smile like a singing sunflower, sweet, potent and bright.

Queen of the forest

I brush the earth with a fleeting glance, mesmerised and in a trance.
The golden-brown trees, this beautiful place where I feel at ease.

I wear my crown, the queen of the forest. A special place to me, the birds sing happily in the trees. A beautiful autumn breeze.

So many creatures great and small. All bound together yet completely different. Alone in my castle, this beautiful and green land.

I dance in the grass, wearing nothing but my crown. Queen of the forest, I walk at peace on the weathered slope. I grab onto the rope of the swing.

Back and forth I go. I feel rested and rejuvenated. I watch the forest around me, it's only beauty that surrounds me. I'm whole and at peace.

Mind at ease

Mind at ease
Heart at peace

I fall asleep on the sand. I wake from my slumber; it grows darker and the distant stars grow brighter. I walk to the shore; ice cold water hits my feet. If water could wash my troubles away, I'd dive into the sea. I sit and watch the blue expanse, how powerful it is. Suddenly storm clouds rumble overhead. I lie back down and rest my head.

Mind at ease
Heart at peace

Sunlit Sky

Standing silently, she smiled

Spinning, spinning sunlit sky

Standing, surrounded
Still, still

Scatter, settle
Sit slowly

Stand, smile sunlit sky

Poets' Retreat

The poets retreat a place to feel free, to sit back and relax and write some poetry. You can come and stay the night or come around for tea. An open space to discuss literature and poetry.

The beach is on the doorstep, let's go sit by the sea. The gulls are calling from up above, the night turns into a party.

A fire is lit, someone rolls up a spliff and stars are dancing rhymical like the sea. Peace enters our bodies; we feel at ease.

The poets retreat, a wonderful place to get the creative juices flowing. Surrounded by such beautiful scenery, one can take a brisk walk beyond the meadows.

Each season has its beauty, we're open all year round. So, jump in your car, the retreats not that far. A place to get creative and make new friends, the fun never ends.

A void inside me

There's always been a void inside me lost and alone with no one beside me.
Like a sense of uncertainty, forever lingering. No one's ever loved me the way I want to be loved. A longing and never quite belonging.

There's always been a voice inside me, telling me I'm unworthy. I tried to relinquish a love that once was, but it was lost at sea. A longing but never quite belonging.

There's always been a misunderstanding people make about me. Yet, you really don't know me, what I've been through. So please don't judge me. A longing but never quite belonging.

There's always been a void inside me, lost and alone with no one to guide me. It will take courage and I need to be stoic. To only count on me, to set myself free. A longing but never belonging. One day I'll belong.

The Oceans Waves

Swirling over the ocean waves, wild horses soaring like the wind.
The sun in my eyes. I'm powerful and free like a bird drifting silently across the sky.

The ghost of you passes by, no more tears left to cry. I smile in the memory of you and me.
Time to move on and set my sail, the ocean blue waits for me.

I finally feel happy and free. I turn and smile as I depart on my new journey.

On a bed of roses

On a bed of roses
Honey -suckled scent.

Love is in the air, when I'm with you
I have no cares.

Relaxed and transfixed
A beautiful sunset.

Our souls connect
On a bed of silk roses, I lie here with you.

Being around nature, nurtures me

Sat here waiting

Sat here waiting, hesitating
Pen and paper in hand, a patient heart.
I write a poem for you.

Longing for the words to come true, to come alive.
Exiled to lonely nights, my lips speak my words of lust for you.

Day and night consumed by you. I want your cigarette kisses
Slip through my fingers and hold me tight. Pen and paper
Still in hand.

Dew on the grass

You cling to me like dew on the grass, I finally had you in my grasp and just for a moment I thought it'd last.

I reminisce on the moments that we shared. The walks we walked, the laughs we shared.
If only you knew just how much I cared.

You cling to me like dew on the grass, yet as I close my eyes, I feel you slipping away.
The memories will forever stay. I know by the way that you kissed me, that somewhere in your heart you'll miss me.

The Rose

Morning light on summer days, an amazing sight through the haze, as I push my way through the long green grass.

A light perfume fills the morning air. Oh, a scent so beautiful it's hard to believe. Aromatic, exotic and a mesmerising sight, as I look forward to this delight.

Like an ocean of discovery, flowers of all colours, pinks, purples, violets and reds. I see some beautiful roses, red perfumed and sweet. Reminding of the last rose you gave to me.

Petals lie besides the flowers, like it's singing me a sweet melody. Our love wasn't meant to be, you left to another city, it was such a pity. You said I'd always be your rose and still love me even when you're old.

A Writer Sacrifice

Brutal honesty
Vulnerability my writing runs away with me. I'm not the woman I used to be.
Writing is my happy place, words I use to replace an empty space.

Writing was once my addiction; it then became an affliction. A writer shows their true
emotions, so to understand me, you really need to listen, listen without judgement.

I'm not perfect, I'm perfectly me. I'm not the woman I used to be, like a caged bird longing to be set free. I write open heartedly like it's my therapy.

Sacrificial ramblings words of honesty. I'm not the woman I used to be. Outside looking in, longing to be free.

You linger everywhere

Take me to Anse d' Azur again and kiss me by the sea.
We can sit and watch the tide come in, it made us so happy.

A summer of love, it danced before our eyes, you were my prize.
A beautiful feeling, I can't disguise.
You linger everywhere.

A light begins to glow

When friends become strangers.
When you look in the mirror and don't recognise yourself anymore.
Losing all hope, struggling to cope.

When family is all you have, and faith becomes your rock.
Thoughts I want to block, time to take stock.

A ray of sunshine a glimpse of hope. The shadows fall back, and a light begins to glow.

Dancing with a poet

Put your arms around me. I'm lost in your eyes; you course through my body. As you dance with me, you entrance me.

Lost in your body, our rhythmic pattern like a line to Saturn, going around and around. Feet lifted off the ground.

Our bodies turning, inside I'm yearning. Our desire is burning, you set my soul on fire. Like I'm performing my words, our moves. Whirling and flirting as we dance the night away.

Petrichor

A hazy summer night, too hot to sleep. It finally rained last night; I walk barefoot outside feet touching the green. The grass a pleasant smell emanating from the soiled earth.

I lay on the grass; the fresh smell permeates around me. My emotions surround me, feeling uplifted. I want to dance, feeling lost and in a trance.

It begins to rain heavily, I don't move. I bask in mother nature's rain. Silence, silence. Once it stops, I smell the aromatic smell of petrichor once again.

Summer Meadow

A beautiful view, a gentle summer breeze.
Lying here I feel at ease.

Wildflowers of all colours, lilacs and creams, yellow and greens.
Splashes of colours dotted around. I lay on the ground listening to the
tranquil sounds. The birds are singing, the bees are buzzing. The sound of the stream trickling lightly in the distance.

I sit and make a daisy chain, it's getting late. I look up at the night sky, its streaked in oranges and reds. I could lie here all night and rest my head.

The thunder of life

Ups and downs
Highs and lows
back and forth, here we go.

Happy and sad
good days and bad.

Heartbreak and sorrow, a better tomorrow.
Falling in love, on a natural high.

Rainy days, storms and showers
Sitting in the garden, surrounded by flowers.
Making love, breaking up
Ups and downs
Highs and lows, sticky Sundays that's how it goes.

Heartbreak hotel, deaths and spells
A long goodbye, a day of desires. One day we shall all be expired.
It's the thunder of life.

A beautiful landscape

Blue, blue the sky is a beautiful view.
I'm here with you, snow white clouds dotted around.
We lie on the golden sand, naked hand in hand.

Green, green the view is serene.
I'm here with you. Kissing underneath a tree, surrounded
by nature, birds singing with glee.

Orange, orange the sunsets on the horizon.
I'm here with you, holding hands underneath the stars.

Red, red we're lying here in bed, kissing and caressing
Lost in your embrace. Bodies entwined, feeling elated.
The moon appears under the pink marbled sky.

Rain, rain it is raining heavily. We run outside wearing
nothing but each other. It's dark, it's wet, yet feels so
exhilarating. I wrap myself around you, feeling safe in your
embrace.

You, you I love the things you do. When I'm with you
there's nothing but blue skies. You bring the best out
Of me. When we are together, I'm happy and free. What
A beautiful landscape we create.

Flower Garden

In hay -sweet evening air, crimson reds dotted around. Beautiful scented flowers on the ground.
The poplar tree sways in the summer grace, it's such a heavenly place.
Swathes of bluebells thick and long. I can hear the birds flutter, in a whirl of colour reds and yellows in the trees, such a beautiful breeze. As summer races away.

Exquisite ecosystem buzzing with amazing creatures. Mother nature adores all her unique features. Viridescent trees accommodate colourful birds. When the wind speaks my soul hears all her words. Scented flowers smile while emanating love. They blossom with help from above, as summer races away.

Collaboration with Chabla Mwape

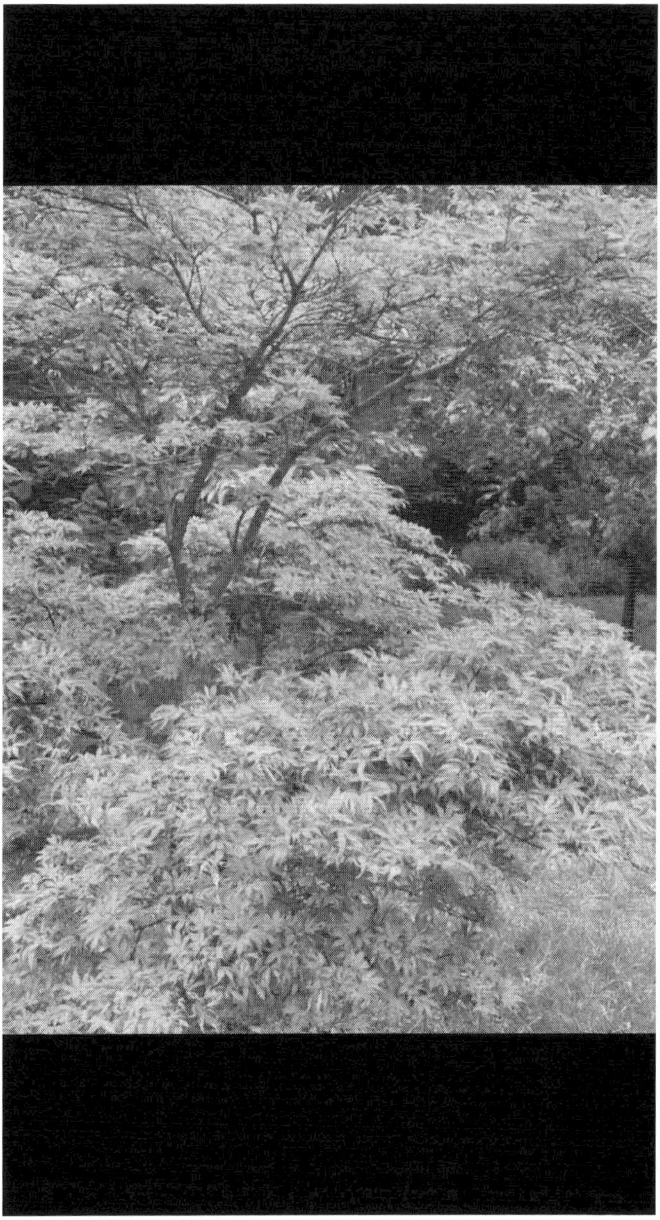

The flowers you once gave me

Whenever I see red roses, they remind me of you and the love we once shared.
You gave me a single rose daily, to show me how much you cared.

You used to buy me a bunch of buttercups, whenever I needed cheering up.
Then for a while it was lilies of the Nile. Once you surprised me with blue tulips
and I gently kissed your lips.

The flowers you once gave me reminds me of you.

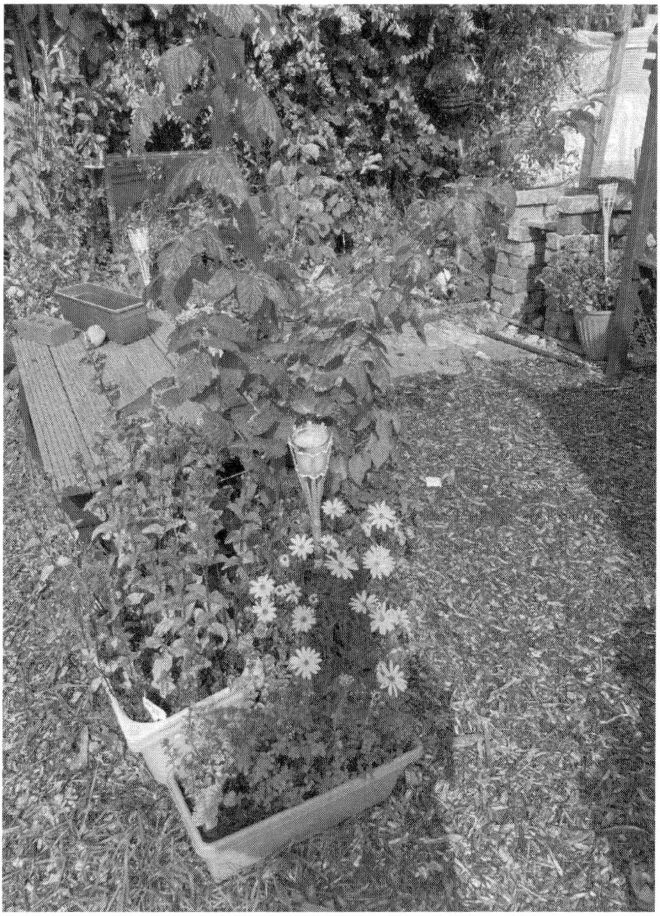

Butterfly Blue

Butterfly blue I'm watching you swirling through the air
Butterfly blue I envy you, I'm mesmerised by your beauty.
So vivid so blue.

Butterfly blue I'm calling to you, I want to have your freedom too.
Butterfly blue I'm watching you, swirling through the air without a care.
Butterfly blue I wish I was you, your beauty so natural it's true.

One day at a time

Sand on my feet, your hand in mine. Star crossed lovers
One day at a time.

Picnic on the beach sipping wine, lovers entwined
One day at a time.

A trip to Paris, a bike ride through Saint Germain
One day at a time.

Late night walks, evening dancing, days at the museum
with passionate kisses
One day at a time.

Gazing into each other's eyes, lazy Sundays in bed
finishing each other's sentences
One day at a time.

Nature's Wild

Nature's wild like mother nature's child.
Early morning wakening, the wind is howling loudly, like kite flying weather.
A strong gust of wind like the raging sound of a howling wolf.

Darkness covers all lands at man's destruction. Plastic and waste sinking into our
Oceans. Surrounded by earths beauty, yet we treat it with cruelty. Like a landfill, waste after waste. Seasons are not seasons anymore.
Natures wild like mother nature's child.

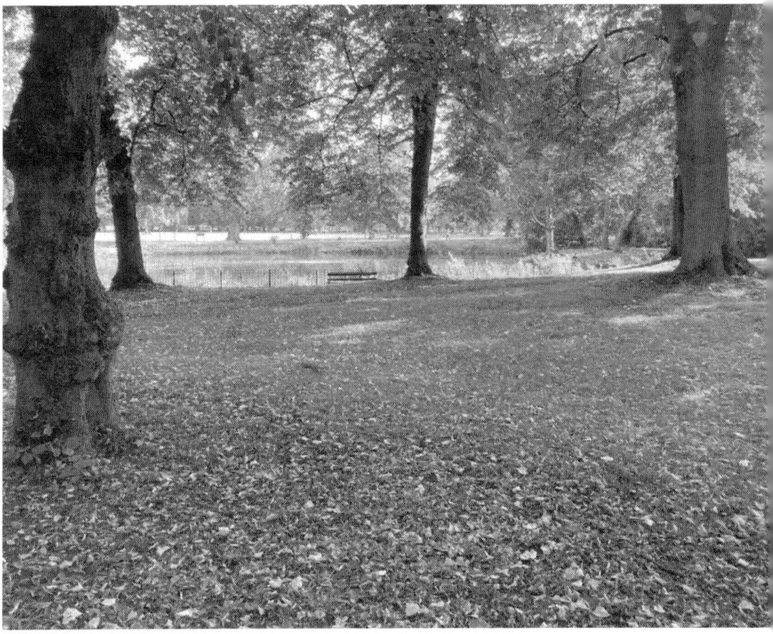

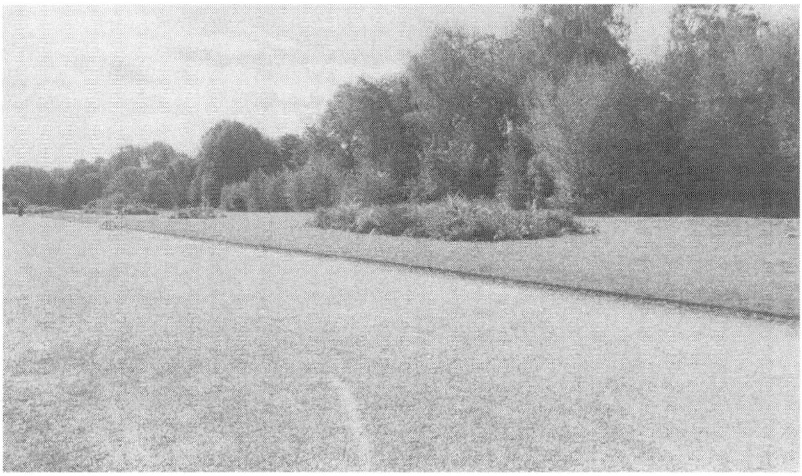

Gratitude

List 5 things you are grateful about

1)

2)

3)

4)

5)

Practice Mindfulness

Walk

Meditate

Dance in the rain

The 4th of May

It is raining today, the 4th of May
Walking through the park, over head
I hear a lark.

I trudge sadly through the woods
And think about the times we shared
they were so good.

My heart lies broken, it's only been
an hour since we've last spoken.
I sit down in solemn silence
I need some friendly guidance.

It's raining today, the 4th of May
The day you took your love away.

Into the woods

A spiritual uplifting, I feel so free as I stand here taking in my surroundings. There's a silence all around me, save for the birds singing high in the trees. Suddenly, I hear a rustling of footsteps. It's you my love.

You walk over and take my hand. I run from you; you chase after me. You finally catch me and hold onto my waist. I can't escape, I don't want to. We laugh like we've never laughed before. We kiss like we've never kissed before. It's just the two of us, into the woods.

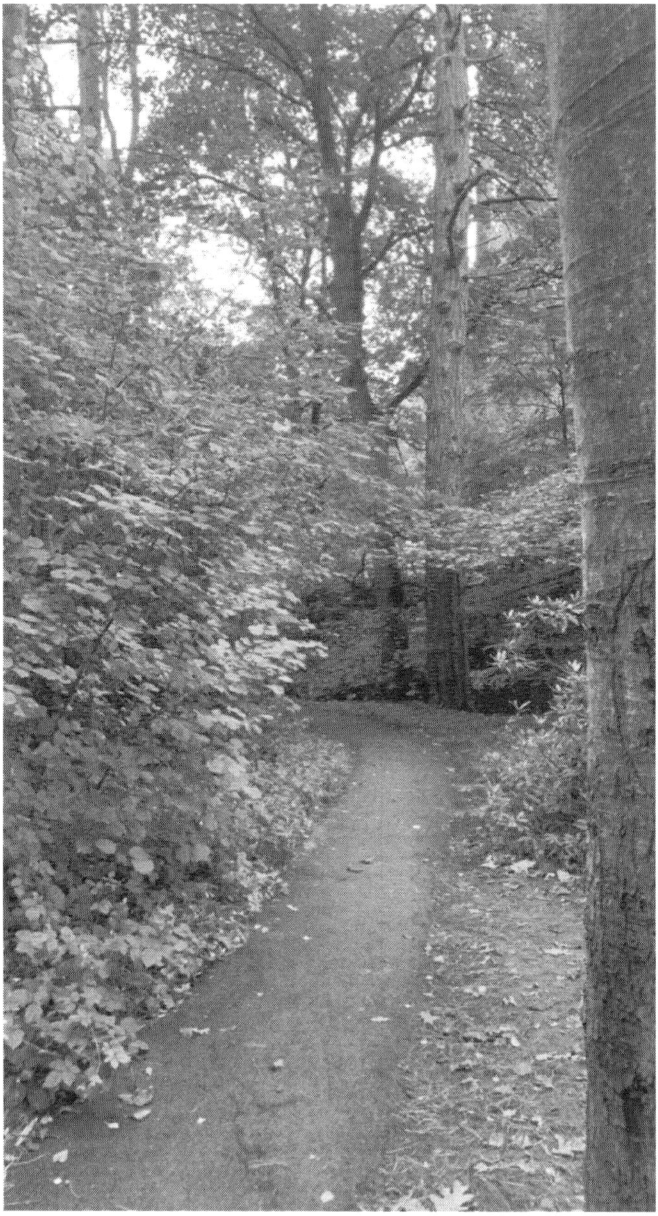

Lavender Fields

We walked through Lavender fields. You kissed me and held me tight
We made sweet love all through the night.

An Autumn Tale

An Autumn tale of love and betrayal.
Stolen moments in the autumn breeze.
Running between trees.
Dancing through the leaves.
The earth sighed; they were caught. Lost in the beginnings of young love.

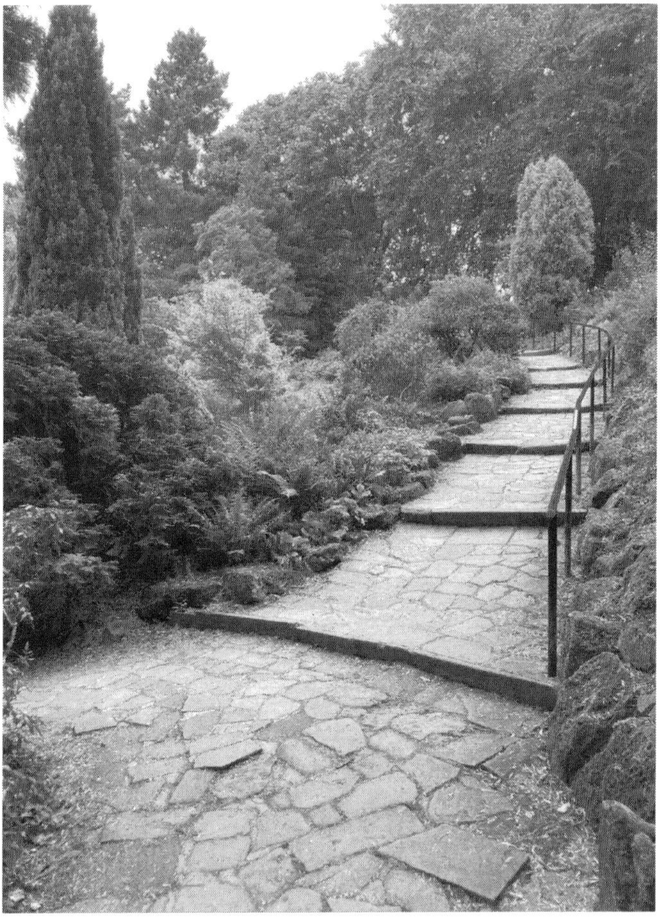

Let me be your light

Let me carry your burdens
Let me hold you tight.

Come lie with me I will protect you; I'll show you the light.
You've been through so much, let me wash away your pain.

Let me carry your burdens
Let me hold you tight.

How they treated you, it wasn't right. Now they've all gone let me show you the light.

Let me carry your burdens
Let me hold you tight.

Let me show you how to love again, to laugh and live.
How to forgive and forget.

Let me carry your burdens
Let me hold you tight.

Let me be the one to nurture you and give you what you need. Let me surround you with happiness, love and laughter.

--------------------, its me your inner self. I'm here for you. Let me help you, you are strong, and you will come through.

Let me carry your burdens
Let me be your light.

You deserve to be happy
You deserve to feel right.

Shades of Blue

The midnight blue sky
Your sea blue eyes
A blue-green waterfall cascading into the aquamarine sea. Waves of blue, dark and emotional. Egyptian blue tulips, the azure stoned ring you once gave to me. Waves of blue because of you. A rainbow of hue, red, violet and blue.

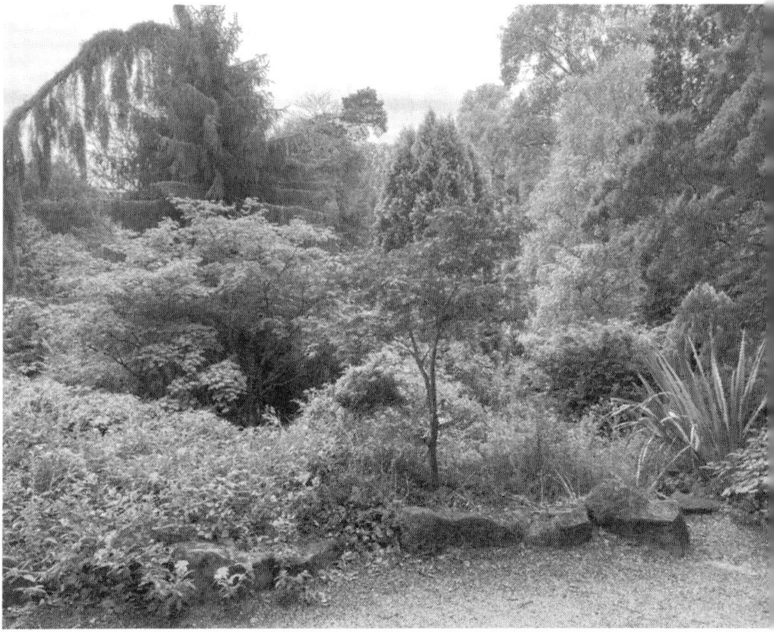

The Weeping Willow

Autumn air the trees stands forlornly
The weeping willow it calls to me, its delicate green
foliage hanging and singing a song.
Weeping willow don't go away as Autumn creeps upon
us. Soon the leaves will be no more.

I sit under the willow tree writing for hours and hours.
Brightly watching the blooming flowers. The words just
flow of the page, I am free and no longer caged. The
grass is soft beneath me soft and green.

I've sat here too long it seems. I watch people passing by,
children laughing, young lovers on a high. I watch the
birds soaring through the sky searching for food as they
pass by. Soon it begins to rain the great old willow tree
shelters me. I feel safe like I'm wrapped up in loving
arms. Birds make their way back to their nests.

Up I get standing alone surrounded by emerald trees. I
drop to my knees, pen still in hand. I go back under the
willow tree and retreat back to writing. I hear the wind
calling in the background, as I look around Autumn
surrounds.

As I write to you

I know what I want to say
What I want to express
Tap, tap, I tap the keys, I read my words out loud.

I feel the morning sun beating down on my face. Delete, delete, the screen is blank once again.

I begin to type again. Once upon a time you were mine. It was all so fine, then you became so unkind. I lost my patience now we are ancient.

From my window a lovely view, I see the park where I met you. Trees and flowers of all different hue. I go back to my laptop and begin to type. I write and I write, about a man I once knew.

Fortress of solitude

Deep in the woods just me, myself and I.
No one to bother me, this is my sanctuary.
I live amongst the animals, they're my friends
I'm the animal whisperer.

I'll dance beneath the marbled moon, content and at
Peace. This comforting landscape, my place to escape
from the rat race. A fast-paced life.

Cosy autumn cocoon I sleep underneath the stars
blanketed by the earth. Dancing in the
thunderstorm, swishing and swirling.
My fortress of solitude.

Nature's wild

Poetic Bliss

Never give a miss to this poetic bliss. I write day and night and despite it all, its my biggest pleasure. Its intoxicating, invigorating and emancipating.

Words pour out from my heart, pen to paper. Sometimes it can only take a moment, I write for my atonement. Its my saving grace, yet my words can't replace your love or embrace. Never give a miss to this poetic bliss. I find solace in writing how I feel. My words are real, an expression of how I feel.

The birds don't sing anymore

Lost inside myself, times of sadness. Having you in my life gave me so much happiness.
Now all I feel is loneliness and the birds don't sing anymore.

Time is supposed to heal how I feel. I pretend I'm okay, getting through each day. It hurts me more than you'll ever know. The birds don't sing anymore.

Friends say it's time to let go, I'll never be the same, all I feel is an emptiness. Lost inside myself and longing for your embrace. The birds don't sing anymore, since you walked out the door.

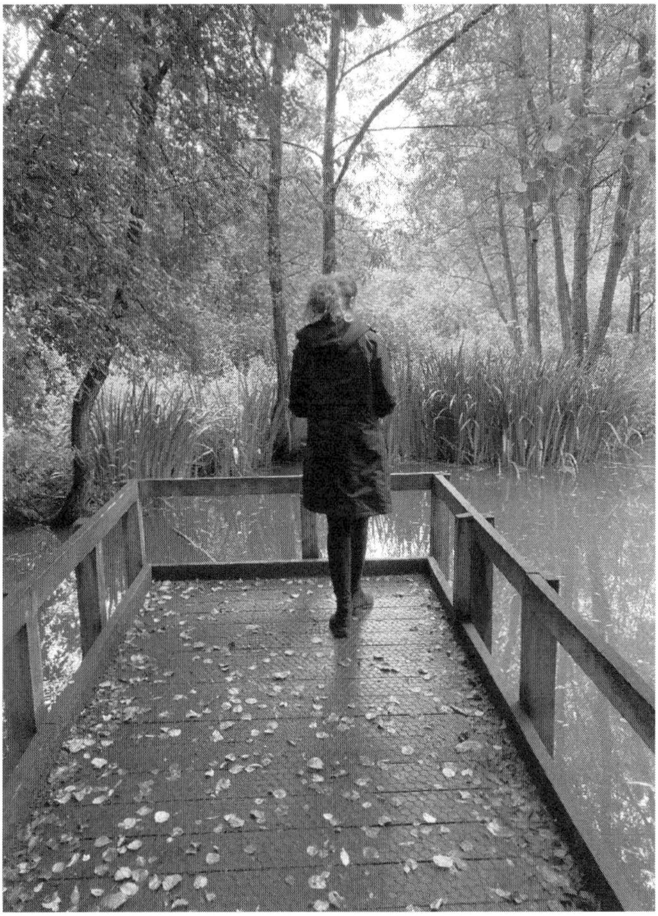

Printed in Great Britain
by Amazon